Cool Caves

THIS EDITION
Editorial Management by Oriel Square
Produced for DK by WonderLab Group LLC
Jennifer Emmett, Erica Green, Kate Hale, *Founders*

Editors Grace Hill Smith, Libby Romero, Maya Myers, Michaela Weglinski;
Photography Editors Kelley Miller, Annette Kiesow, Nicole di Mella; **Managing Editor** Rachel Houghton;
Designers Project Design Company; **Researcher** Michelle Harris; **Copy Editor** Lori Merritt;
Indexer Connie Binder; **Proofreader** Larry Shea; **Reading Specialist** Dr. Jennifer Albro;
Curriculum Specialist Elaine Larson

Published in the United States by DK Publishing
1745 Broadway, 20th Floor, New York, NY 10019

Copyright © 2023 Dorling Kindersley Limited
DK, a Division of Penguin Random House LLC
24 25 26 27 28 10 9 8 7 6 5 4 3 2 1
001–341825–Mar/2024

A catalog record for this book
is available from the Library of Congress.
ISBN: 978-0-5938-4255-3

DK books are available at special discounts when purchased in bulk for sales promotions, premiums,
fundraising, or educational use. For details, contact: DK Publishing Special Markets,
1745 Broadway, 20th Floor, New York, NY 10019
SpecialSales@dk.com

Printed and bound in China

The publisher would like to thank the following for their kind permission to reproduce their images:
a=above; c=center; b=below; l=left; r=right; t=top; b/g=background

Alamy Stock Photo: agefotostock / Sami Sarkis 23b, Natalia Pryanishnikova 12-13b, Westend61 GmbH / Martin Siepmann 14,
Rudmer Zwerver 27br; **Dreamstime.com:** Aiisha 17, Dslaven 19cra, Sandra Foyt 11br, Kateryna Kon 25br, Julia Kuznetsova 1cb,
Olena Lysytsia 20crb, Manon14 18–19t, Suse Schulz 13crb, Sjors737 9br; **Getty Images:** 500px / Christopher Cullen 20br,
Corbis Documentary / Douglas Peebles 22b, Photodisc / Nancy Nehring 11t; **Getty Images / iStock:** MarcelStrelow 26t,
milehightraveler 6-7; **NASA:** JPL 23tl; **Science Photo Library:** Javier Trueba / MSF 3cb, 24t; **Shutterstock.com:** Aerial-motion 28-29,
Altosvic 21, Ales Cesen 16br, kid315 8t, ouran 8tl (pointer), 10tr (pointer), 13tr (pointer), 15tr (pointer), 17tl (pointer), 18tl (pointer),
21tr (pointer), 22tr (pointer), 24tl (pointer), 27tr (pointer), Soloma 8tl (Globe), 10tr (Globe), 13tr (Globe), 15tr (Globe), 17tl (Globe),
18tl (Globe), 21tr (Globe), 22tr (Globe), 24tl (Globe), 27tr (Globe), Vladimir Shutter 15bl, Sigit Adhi Wibowo 4-5

Cover images: *Front:* **Dreamstime.com:** Rixie

All other images © Dorling Kindersley
For more information see: www.dkimages.com

www.dk.com

MIX
Paper | Supporting
responsible forestry
FSC™ C018179

This book was made with Forest
Stewardship Council™ certified
paper – one small step in DK's
commitment to a sustainable future.
**For more information go to
www.dk.com/our-green-pledge**

Level 3

Cool Caves

Libby Romero

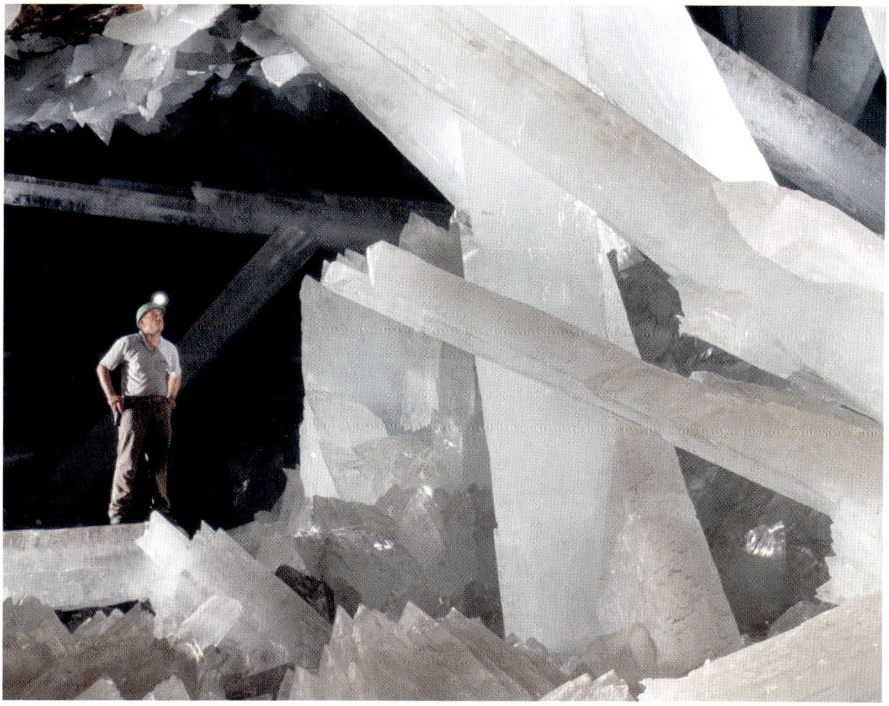

DK

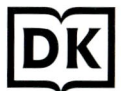

Contents

Discovering Caves

Come on in! It's dark. It's chilly. And it's very quiet inside a cave. It's so quiet that you can hear bats flying, insects crawling, and water dripping down from the surface above. Sounds bounce off the walls and echo throughout the hollow chamber. The total darkness makes them seem louder than they really are.

Carlsbad Caverns
New Mexico, USA

Caves are a part of nature. They can be found underground, in hillsides, or on the sides of cliffs. There are caves inside glaciers and hardened lava, too. Caves can be pretty cool!

Some caves are smaller than a classroom. Others are so big that entire city blocks could fit inside them. Many caves have an opening large enough for a person to pass through. And every cave has a chamber that goes back farther than sunlight can filter in. Within that dark space lies a world of creatures and features just waiting to be explored.

Son Doong Cave

Son Doong Cave in Vietnam is the world's largest cave. It wasn't discovered until 1990. A local man found it after he saw clouds billowing from its opening. When he got closer, he heard the sounds of a raging river coming from inside. He couldn't wait to show someone the cave he had found.

Unfortunately, the cave is hidden in the middle of a jungle, and it took the man 18 years to find that opening again! When he did, he guided explorers to the cave.

Inside, two rivers join together and flow along a fault line—a large crack in Earth's surface. That's why the cave's passages are so huge.

Deep in the cave, the explorers found rainforests growing from the cave's floor. The cave ceiling had collapsed to create two giant openings. Sunlight shines through the openings to the plants and trees below.

Mighty Large
Son Doong Cave, which means "mountain river cave," formed about three million years ago. The main cavern is so big that an entire city block of 40-story skyscrapers could fit inside its chamber.

Mammoth Cave

Mammoth Cave is the world's longest cave system. It lies beneath the woodlands of central Kentucky in the United States. The cave started to form 10 to 15 million years ago. Rainwater seeped through cracks in limestone rock. It combined with carbon dioxide to create a weak acid. The acid dissolved the rocks. This is how most caves form. They are called solution caves.

Flowing water created five levels of passageways inside Mammoth Cave. Dripping water combined with minerals to create lots of different cave formations, such as stalactites and stalagmites.

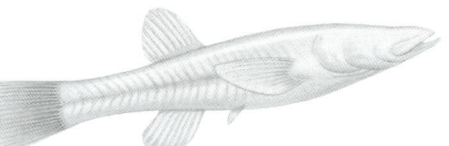

The northern cavefish lives inside Mammoth Cave. The fish is white and has no eyes. It has adapted over time to live in total darkness.

Stalactites hang down from the ceiling. Stalagmites rise up from the floor. Sheets of minerals form curtain-shaped deposits called flowstone along the cave's walls. Little knobs called cave popcorn grow in the cave, too. Can you guess how they got their name?

Carlsbad Caverns

Carlsbad Caverns in New Mexico, USA, are solution caves, too. But these caves formed in a different way. Gases from oil deposits in the ground and tiny microbes combined with oxygen in the air, creating an acid that dissolved the rocks.

Sac Actun Cave System

The second-longest cave system in the world is Sac Actun. It lies along the Caribbean coast in Mexico's Yucatán Peninsula. It's a bit harder to explore these passageways—they're underwater! To enter, divers plunge into a deep sinkhole called a cenote. There are more than 220 cenotes within the Sac Actun system.

Sac Actun's passageways weren't always underwater. Deep inside, divers have found hidden treasures that reveal clues about the past. There are ceramics, drawings on cave walls, and even a shrine to the Mayan god of war and commerce. Divers have also found the remains of ancient humans. There are bones of animals, like saber-toothed tigers, too.

Ancient Mayans considered caves to be sacred places—especially the Sac Actun caves that led to water.

Lascaux Cave

Another cave that has taught us about the past is the Lascaux Cave in France. Around 600 paintings, mostly of animals, and 1,400 engravings decorate the cave's walls. The artwork was created around 17,000 to 15,000 BCE.

Eisriesenwelt Cave

Frozen water, or ice, is what makes the Eisriesenwelt Cave in the Austrian Alps so spectacular. It is an ice cave. An ice cave is a cave formed in stone that has ice in it all year long.

Because of how air moves through the lower parts of this cave, the temperature is always freezing there. As water drips in, it freezes to create fantastic ice sculptures. Eisriesenwelt is the largest ice cave in the world. Some of the ice in it is about 1,000 years old.

Giant Ice

Eisriesenwelt is a German word. It means "world of ice giants." Inside the cave, there are stalactites, stalagmites, domes, and even waterfalls made out of ice.

Crystal Cave

Glacier caves are often mistakenly called ice caves. But these caves actually form inside glaciers. There are lots of glacier caves in Iceland. Crystal Cave in the Vatnajökull Glacier is one of the most famous. It is on Iceland's coast.

Ice on the walls and ceiling of this cave is a beautiful aquamarine blue. The ice on its floor is nearly black. The walls are smooth, especially the farther in you go. And the passages are narrow. That makes it easy to hear the glacier pop and crackle as it moves.

Safety First

During summer, glacier caves melt. Often, they collapse. That's why these caves can only be explored during winter, when the ice is frozen and the caves are stable. It's also why you should only enter these caves with an experienced guide.

Marble Caves

The Marble Caves, rising along General Carrera Lake in Chile, are some of the most beautiful caves in the world. Over the past 6,000 years, waves pounding the pure marble cliffs have sculpted the caves. The caves have smooth, curved walls. They are lined with swirling patterns of blue.

Sea Caves

Although they're on a lake, the Marble Caves are sea caves. Sea caves form in cliffs that line an ocean or lake. Waves break down the rock as they smash into the coast.

The blue color is a reflection. It comes from glacial water in the lake. The shade of blue changes depending on the lake's water level and the time of year. In spring, when water levels are lower, the walls are bright turquoise. In summer, when the water is deeper, the walls are a dark navy blue.

Fingal's Cave

The walls of Fingal's Cave on Scotland's Staffa Island are lined with massive six-sided columns of basalt. Basalt is a type of volcanic rock. According to legend, the cave is the work of a giant. It is one end of a bridge that the giant built so he could cross from Ireland to Scotland to fight another giant.

In reality, the rocky columns were formed by lava that flowed and cooled about 60 million years ago. Ocean waves, chipping away at the rocks, created the cave over time.

Pleasant Tune
Fingal's Cave is also known for its music. The sound of the waves bounces off the cave's arched roof. This produces a beautiful melody.

Kazumura Cave

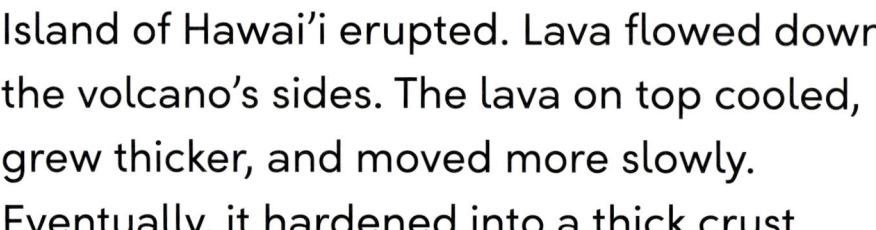

Around 500 years ago, the Kīlauea volcano on the Big Island of Hawai'i erupted. Lava flowed down the volcano's sides. The lava on top cooled, grew thicker, and moved more slowly. Eventually, it hardened into a thick crust.

Hotter, faster lava flowed like a river beneath the crust. It formed a tube as the lava kept flowing underneath the cooled top. When the eruption stopped, the lava drained out of the tube.

hot lava flowing inside a lava tube

Lunar Lava Tubes

Scientists think there are lava tubes on the Moon, too. If so, they may be good places to build lunar bases. An underground base would protect astronauts from meteoroid strikes and huge changes in temperature.

As the tube cooled, a tunnel formed inside. It stretches for more than 40 miles (64 km). This is the Kazumura Cave, which is thought to be the longest lava tube in the world.

Cave of Crystals

In the year 2000, miners in Mexico discovered the Cave of Crystals. It is one of the most unusual caves on Earth. Shaped like a horseshoe, the cave is filled with giant crystals. Some of the crystals are more than 36 feet (11 m) tall and 3.2 feet (1 m) thick.

Scientists believe that groundwater flooded the cave about 500,000 years ago. A pool of magma heated it from below. The hot water came in contact with cool water from above, and crystals began to grow. The water's temperature held steady, so the crystals kept growing.

Though the cave is beautiful, it is dangerous. When researchers explore inside, they can only stay for a short time. Temperatures in the cave can rise up to 136°F (58°C). And the relative humidity stays around 100 percent. The heat and the humidity can be deadly, as the moisture in the air can condense in a person's lungs.

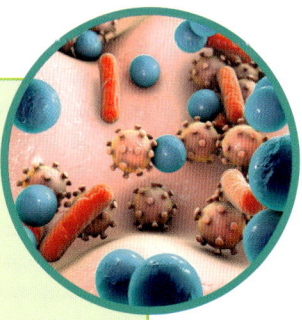

Tiny Life
Scientists found tiny microbes in the Cave of Crystals that have been dormant for up to 50,000 years! There is nothing else like them on Earth.

Waitomo Caves

Long ago, powerful underground streams cut through layers of limestone in New Zealand. This created the Waitomo cave system. The caves are cool, but it's what lives inside that sparks people's imaginations—literally!

The Waitomo Caves are filled with glowworms. These larvae of a species of gnat look like maggots. Their tails are bioluminescent. They contain chemicals that react with oxygen to produce an eerie blue light.

That blue glow is beautiful to humans. But it has a deadly purpose. It attracts other insects. The glowworms spin a sticky thread that hangs down from the cave roof. When prey approaches the light, it gets stuck in the thread. Just like a spider's web, the glowworm's thread captures a meal.

Cave Crickets

Glowworms get all the attention, but other animals live in the Waitomo Caves, too—including the Waitomo cave weta. These big cave crickets have been around since the days of the dinosaurs. They gather near cave openings during the day and come out at night to eat.

No matter how a cave was formed or what you can find inside, caves are fascinating places to explore. They may be dark. They may be damp. They may hold creatures you've never seen before.

Some caves have been around for thousands or even millions of years. They hold secrets to Earth's past. They reveal clues about how people once lived. They show how animals evolved over time. Caves are pretty cool. Wouldn't you agree?

Glossary

Bioluminescent
[by-oh-loo-min-ESS-ent]
Able to give off light as a living organism, such as a firefly

Cave
A natural underground chamber that has an opening to the surface

Cenote
[si-NO-tay]
A deep sinkhole filled with water

Chamber
A large room

Crystal
A substance that forms a pattern of many flat surfaces when it becomes a solid

Fault line
A large crack in Earth's surface

Flowstone
Minerals deposited by a thin sheet of water along the walls or floor of a cave

Glacier
A large mass of slowly moving ice

Glowworm
A worm-shaped insect that can produce and give off light from its body

Hollow
Having an unfilled space inside

Lava
Hot, molten rock that comes out of an erupting volcano and hardens as it cools

Magma
Molten rock found beneath Earth's surface that forms lava when it flows out of volcanoes

Stalactite
[stuh-LACK-tite]
A deposit of minerals that hangs down from the roof or sides of a cave

Stalagmite
[stuh-LAG-mite]
A deposit of minerals that builds up from a cave floor

Index

Quiz

Answer the questions to see what you have learned. Check your answers in the key below.

1. Where is the world's largest cave?

2. What is the most common type of cave on Earth?

3. What is the difference between a stalactite and a stalagmite?

4. Why is it difficult to explore the Sac Actun cave system?

5. What kind of cave is the Eisriesenwelt Cave in the Austrian Alps?

6. What do the Marble Caves in Chile and Fingal's Cave in Scotland have in common?

7. What did miners discover in a cave in Mexico?

8. What are the Waitomo Caves in New Zealand known for?

1. Vietnam 2. A solution cave 3. Stalactites hang down from a cave ceiling and stalagmites rise up from the floor 4. It is underwater 5. An ice cave 6. Both were formed by waves 7. Giant crystals 8. Glowworms

DINOSAURS
DISCOVERED

DK | Penguin Random House

FIRST EDITION

Editors Katy Lennon, Kritika Gupta, Abhijit Dutta; **Project Art Editors** Emma Hobson, Yamini Panwar; **Art Editor** Shubham Rohatgi; **US Editor** Jennette ElNaggar; **US Senior Editor** Shannon Beatty; **Jacket Coordinator** Francesca Young; **Jacket Designer** Dheeraj Arora; **DTP Designers** Dheeraj Singh, Mohd Rizwan; **Picture Researcher** Sakshi Saluja; **Producer, Pre-Production** Dragana Puvacic; **Producer** Barbara Ossawska; **Managing Editors** Laura Gilbert, Monica Saigal; **Managing Art Editor** Diane Peyton Jones; **Deputy Managing Art Editor** Ivy Sengupta; **Delhi Team Head** Malavika Talukder; **Creative Director** Helen Senior; **Publishing Director** Sarah Larter; **Reading Consultant** Linda Gambrell, PhD; **Educational Consultant** Jacqueline Harris

THIS EDITION

Editorial Management by Oriel Square
Produced for DK by WonderLab Group LLC
Jennifer Emmett, Erica Green, Kate Hale, *Founders*

Editors Grace Hill Smith, Libby Romero, Michaela Weglinski; **Photography Editors** Kelley Miller, Annette Kiesow, Nicole DiMella; **Managing Editor** Rachel Houghton; **Designers** Project Design Company; **Researcher** Michelle Harris; **Copy Editor** Lori Merritt; **Indexer** Connie Binder; **Proofreader** Larry Shea; **Reading Specialist** Dr. Jennifer Albro; **Curriculum Specialist** Elaine Larson

Published in the United States by DK Publishing
1745 Broadway, 20th Floor, New York, NY 10019

Copyright © 2023 Dorling Kindersley Limited
DK, a Division of Penguin Random House LLC
24 25 26 27 28 10 9 8 7 6 5 4 3 2 1
001–341825–Mar/2024

A catalog record for this book
is available from the Library of Congress.
ISBN: 978-0-5938-4255-3

DK books are available at special discounts when purchased in bulk for sales promotions, premiums, fundraising, or educational use. For details, contact: DK Publishing Special Markets, 1745 Broadway, 20th Floor, New York, NY 10019
SpecialSales@dk.com

Printed and bound in China

The publisher would like to thank the following for their kind permission to reproduce their images:
a=above; c=center; b=below; l=left; r=right; t=top; b/g=background

123RF.com: alexeykonovalenko 6–7bc, leonello calvetti 37tc; **Alamy Stock Photo:** Javier Etcheverry 43, GL Archive 20cl, Stocktrek Images, Inc. / Nobumichi Tamura 22–23b; **Dorling Kindersley:** Andy Crawford / Robert L. Braun 37cra, Andy Crawford / Royal Tyrrell Museum of Palaeontology, Alberta, Canada 8, Andy Crawford Courtesy of Dorset Dinosaur Museum 9b; **Getty Images:** Science Photo Library / Roger Harris 20–21; **Shutterstock.com:** Dew_gdragon 9t

Cover images: *Front:* **Dorling Kindersley:** Jon Hughes bc; **Dreamstime.com:** Mark Turner c; **Shutterstock.com:** Herschel Hoffmeyer

All other images © Dorling Kindersley
For more information see: www.dkimages.com

www.dk.com

MIX
Paper | Supporting
responsible forestry
FSC™ C018179

This book was made with Forest Stewardship Council™ certified paper - one small step in DK's commitment to a sustainable future. **For more information go to www.dk.com/our-green-pledge**

Level 3

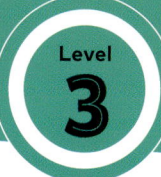

DINOSAURS DISCOVERED

Dean R. Lomax

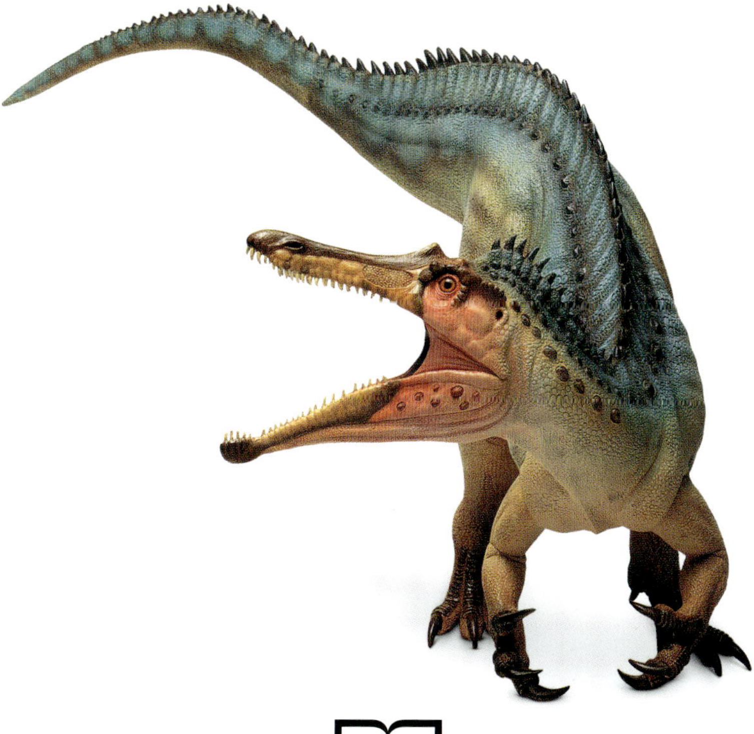

DK

Contents

Who Studies Dinosaurs?

From deserts to mountains, dinosaur bones are found all around the world. Each new dinosaur discovery has its own story to tell about how and where these prehistoric animals lived.

Scientists who study dinosaurs look for their fossils. Fossils are the remains of animals and plants that have been left in rocks. They can be millions of years old and can give us clues about the history of our planet. From fossils, scientists can find out what dinosaurs ate, how big they were, and even what color they were.

coprolites, or fossilized dinosaur poop

A team of scientists called paleontologists at an excavation site

For a dinosaur to become a fossil, it must have died in special conditions. Many fossils are created when an animal dies close to (or in) water. It then becomes buried by mud or sand at the bottom of the water. Over time, the soft parts of its body rot away, leaving just the hard parts, such as bones and teeth.

As the skeleton is buried deeper, minerals from the watery mud get into the bones. The mud hardens into rock. The bones harden, too, creating a fossil.

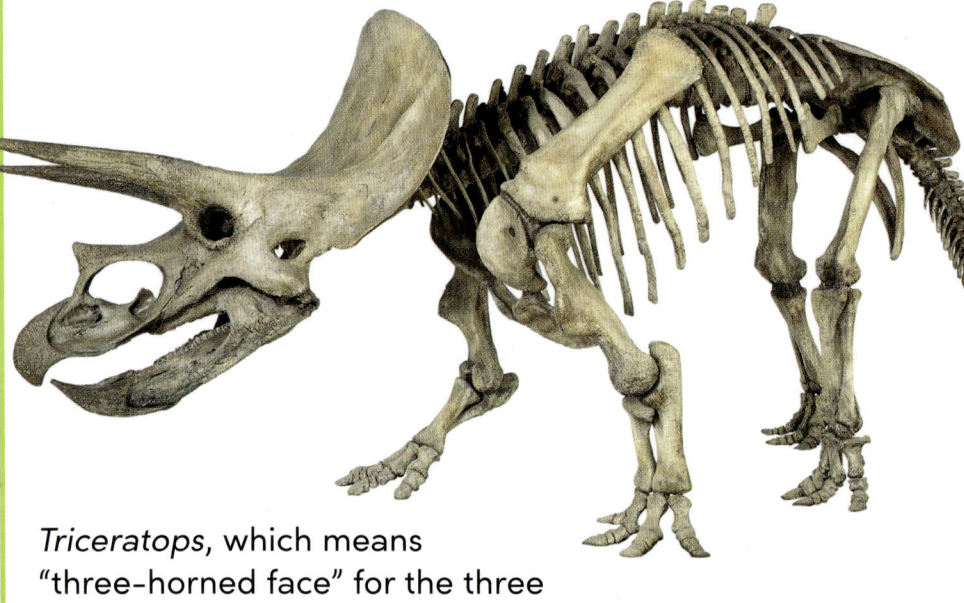

Triceratops, which means "three-horned face" for the three horns on the dinosaur's skull

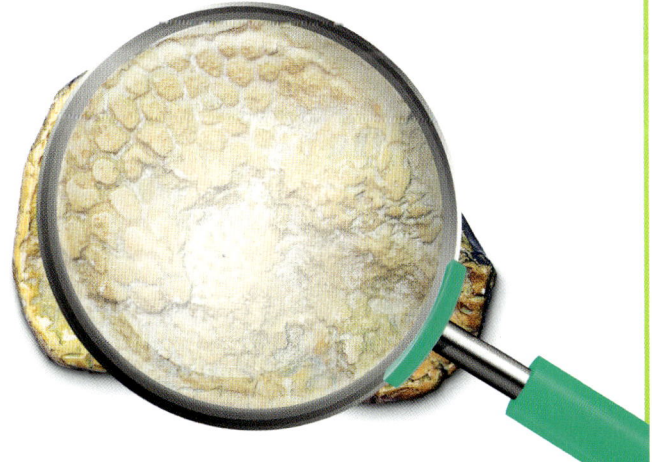

Naming Dinosaurs

On average, scientists discover a new species of dinosaur every week! When they find a new dinosaur, they get to name it. Dinosaur names are taken from Greek or Latin words. Dinosaurs are often named for a feature, such as sharp teeth or horns. Others are named after the place they were discovered or the person who found them.

fossilized dinosaur skin

Dinosaur Discoveries

Here are some of the most important events in the study of dinosaurs.

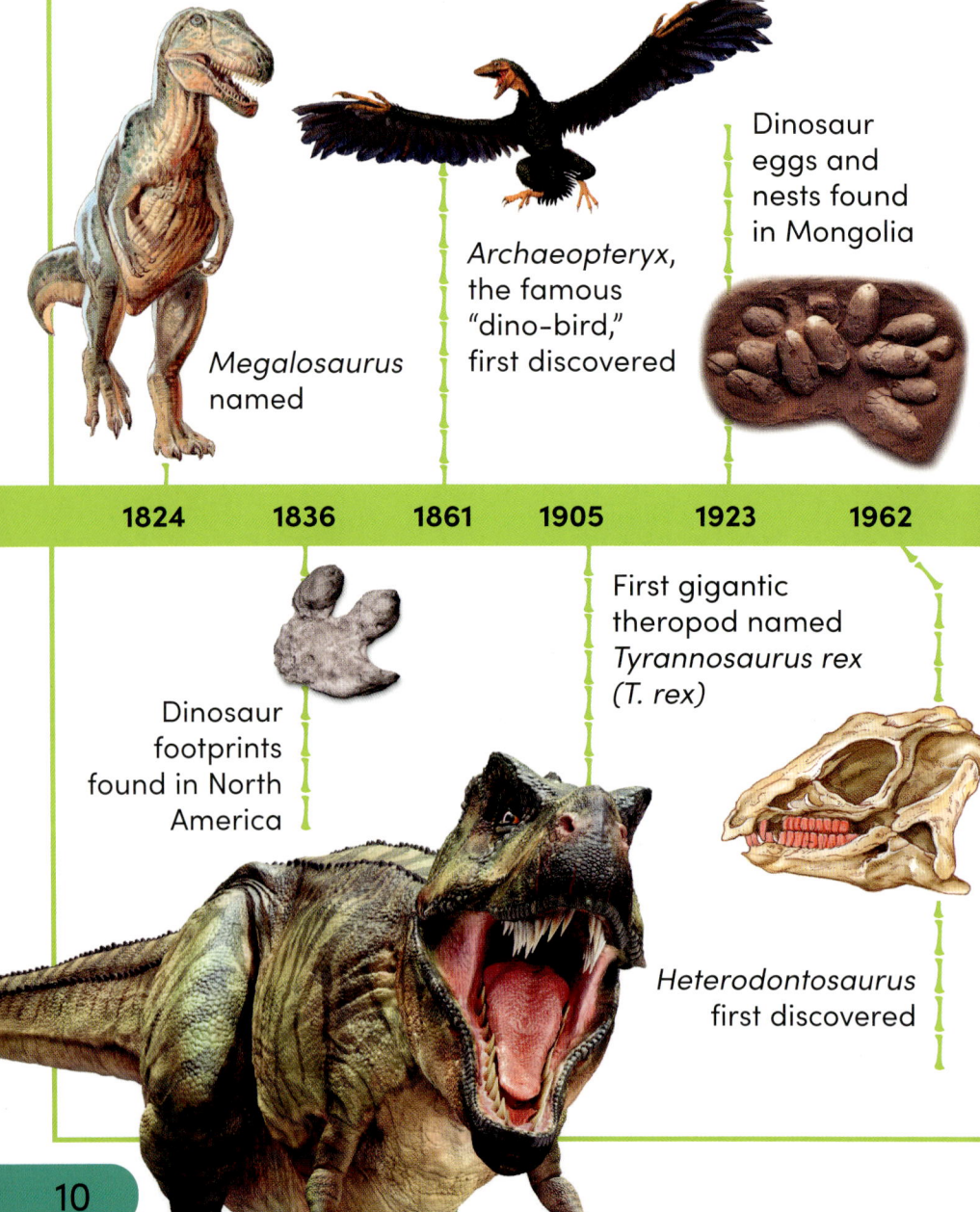

Archaeopteryx, the famous "dino-bird," first discovered

Dinosaur eggs and nests found in Mongolia

Megalosaurus named

1824 1836 1861 1905 1923 1962

Dinosaur footprints found in North America

First gigantic theropod named *Tyrannosaurus rex* (T. rex)

Heterodontosaurus first discovered

The gigantic *Argentinosaurus* is named; it is the largest dinosaur discovered so far

Scientists suggest that a comet or asteroid struck Earth about 66 million years ago, wiping out the nonbird dinosaurs

One of the world's richest dinosaur graveyards is found in Canada

| 1979 | 1980 | 1990 | 1993 | 1997 | 2016 |

An important study shows that dinosaurs cared for their young

The world's most complete *T. rex* is discovered and nicknamed "Sue"

Part of a dinosaur tail with feathers is found in amber

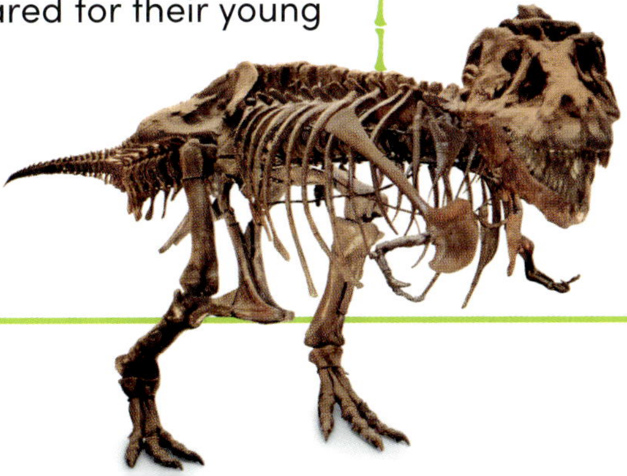

Dinosaur Map

Dinosaurs lived all over the globe. Here is a map to show where some of them came from.

USA

NORTH AMERICA

UK

Tyrannosaurus

Eoraptor

SOUTH AMERICA

ARGENTINA

Giganotosaurus

Velociraptor

Megalosaurus

EUROPE

MONGOLIA

ASIA

Spinosaurus

CHINA

EGYPT

Microraptor

AFRICA

TANZANIA

AUSTRALIA

Giraffatitan

Leaellynasaura

Cryolophosaurus

ANTARCTICA

13

Wonders of Europe

Many early dinosaur discoveries were made in Europe. One of the most important was the "dino-bird," which was found in Germany in 1861. It had a long, bony tail, sharp teeth, and feathers. It was one of the first fossils to show a close link between birds and dinosaurs. Today, scientists place birds and dinosaurs in the same family.

"dino-bird," or
Archaeopteryx

A skeleton of an *Iguanodon*, the type of dinosaur unearthed in Belgium

Nearby, deep inside a Belgian coal mine in 1878, another amazing discovery was made. A herd of more than 30 dinosaur skeletons were found together. It is thought that they all fell down a ravine and drowned when it flooded.

In Portugal many years later, scientists found fossilized dinosaur eggs. The eggs even had unborn babies preserved inside them.

Baryonyx's claw

In 1983, a fossil collector was looking for fossils in a quarry in England. He found an unusual rock, which contained a large claw.

Scientists visited the site and found more than half of the dinosaur's skeleton, including a large skull with teeth in it. It was said to be the find of the century.

The dinosaur lived about 125 million years ago, but its last meal was still preserved in its stomach. It had eaten a tasty meal of fish and other dinosaurs.

Baryonyx walkeri, named after William Walker, the fossil collector who discovered the dinosaur's fossilized claw in a quarry

One dinosaur that lived on an island off the coast of Germany was part of a family of dinosaurs that were the largest dinosaurs to ever walk Earth.

The first bones of this island dinosaur were found in the mid–1990s. Scientists studied them closely. The bones showed a surprise. They were smaller than expected.

These dinosaurs didn't grow as large as those of other dinosaurs in the same family because there wasn't much food for them to eat on their small island.

An *Europasaurus,*
a smaller version
of its relatives

One group of large dinosaurs, called stegosaurs, had bony plates along their backs and spikes on their tails. The first skeleton in this group to be discovered was found in England in 1874. It had leg bones, armor plates, and tail spines. Its name, *Dacentrurus*, means "very pointy tail."

Discovering Dinosaurs

Famous scientist Sir Richard Owen identified this creature with a pointy tail as a new dinosaur. In fact, Owen was the scientist who coined the word "dinosaur." In 1842, he gave these giant reptiles that once roamed Earth their own name. An expert on animal skeletons, Owen learned that dinosaurs were not just large lizards. They were a separate group of animals.

Stegosaurus

Digging in Asia

The first nonbird dinosaur found with feathers was discovered in China in 1996. This find was more proof that birds and dinosaurs are part of the same family.

One of these dinosaurs was very well preserved. Scientists could even tell what color it was. It was reddish brown and had camouflage patterns and stripes.

The turkey-size *Sinosauropteryx*, the first nonbird dinosaur found with feathers

A *Protoceratops*, the type of dinosaur found buried in the Gobi desert

fossil of a *Sinosauropteryx*

Another exciting dinosaur discovery was made in the Gobi desert. In 1971, scientists dug out fossils of two dinosaurs fighting. The battle had become frozen in time as the pair were buried by sand, possibly from the collapse of a sand dune.

In 2002, scientists visited a desert-like area in China. They found two small skeletons. One of the skeletons belonged to an adult. The other was around 6 years old when it died. The dinosaur was an early ancestor of the *T. rex*. It had a large crest on its head. The crest may have been brightly colored. It could have been used to attract a mate.

Named *Guanlong*,
or "crowned dragon,"
for its head crest

In 1965, a team of scientists found part of a skeleton in the Gobi desert. It had huge arms with powerful claws. Its name means "terrible hand." The missing bones made it difficult for the team to know what the dinosaur looked like.

Deinocheirus claw

The ostrich-like *Deinocheirus*; scientists think its wide toe claws kept it from sinking into muddy riverbanks.

It was thought to have been a giant meat eater that walked on two legs. For almost 50 years, it remained one of the most mysterious dinosaurs ever discovered.

In 2014, the mystery behind the giant claws was solved! Two more skeletons were found. The dinosaur was the largest member of the ostrich-like group of dinosaurs.

Days of the Dinosaurs

Dinosaurs flourished for more than 165 million years. This time was split into three periods. Follow the lines to match the dinosaurs to when they lived.

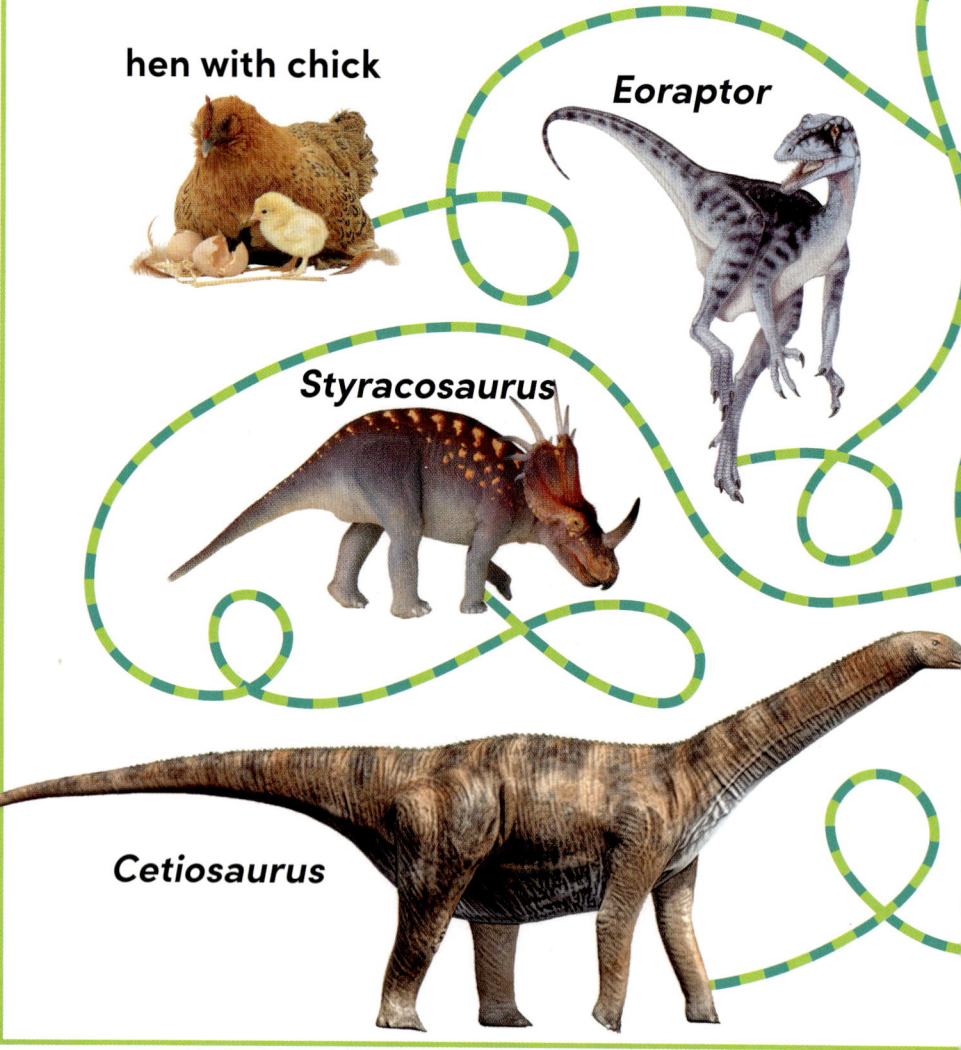

hen with chick

Eoraptor

Styracosaurus

Cetiosaurus

Triassic Period

This period was 252 to 201 million years ago. The first dinosaurs appeared around 231 million years ago.

Jurassic Period

This period was 201 to 145 million years ago. Some of the largest dinosaurs first appeared at this time.

Cretaceous Period

The last of the nonbird dinosaurs died during this period 145 to 66 million years ago.

Today

There are dinosaurs alive today—they are birds!

African Adventures

A lot of dinosaur fossils have been collected from all across Africa. In 1976, a cluster of six eggs was found in South Africa. Five eggs still contained unborn babies. The eggs belonged to a plant-eating dinosaur.

Another dinosaur found in Africa could live in and out of water and had large spines on its back. The spines formed a sail or hump. This sail may have been used for display or defense, or to help the dinosaur control its temperature.

An almost complete embryo, or unborn baby, of *Massospondylus*

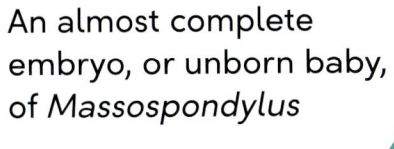

A *Spinosaurus* with its crocodile-like mouth and large sail sticking out of the water

There are many large animals alive today, but none as tall as a dinosaur found in Tanzania.

It was one of the tallest dinosaurs ever and was twice the height of a giraffe. That's why its name means "giant giraffe." And also like giraffes, they used their long necks to eat leaves from the treetops.

It was also one of the heaviest dinosaurs. It weighed about the same as five adult African elephants!

A wandering herd of long-necked *Giraffatitans*

Skeleton of *Heterodontosaurus*

In South Africa, between 1961 and 1962, a team of scientists found a skull, a jaw, and some teeth that belonged to an interesting dinosaur.

It was about the size of a fox. It belonged to
a family of dinosaurs that had special teeth.
Most dinosaurs had lots of the same type
of tooth in their mouths. But these
dinosaurs had different kinds
of teeth. This suggests that
they may have eaten both
plants and animals.

This fox-size dinosaur may have
had coarse bristles on its skin.

Giants of America

Many dinosaur discoveries in the Americas have helped us understand a lot about how these animals lived. The largest dinosaur and the oldest dinosaur were both found in South America!

Dinosaur Discoveries

The area that is now North America was once home to some incredible dinosaurs. *Tyrannosaurus* (left), *Triceratops* (middle), and *Stegosaurus* (right) were just a few that lived there.

Argentinosaurus, the largest dinosaur that ever lived

The group of dinosaurs that are often called raptors were fast. They had sharp teeth and claws. Many species were quite small—about the size of a turkey. In 2005, part of a skeleton was found in South Dakota. Ten years later, the bones were identified as a new species. This dinosaur was almost twice as long as a polar bear, making it one of the largest raptor dinosaurs known.

Named *Dakotaraptor* after where its skeleton was found, this dinosaur probably used its feathers to keep warm.

raptor dinosaur claw

It lived at the same time and in the same area as the giant *T. rex*. Bumps were found on the arm bones of the skeleton. These are called quill knobs. They suggest that this dinosaur had feathers.

In 2011, news broke that an exciting fossil had been uncovered in Canada. Scientists visited the site. They were amazed to find that the skeleton was an almost complete armored dinosaur.

It is so well preserved that the 110-million-year-old fossil looks as if it is sleeping. Bits of color were even found in its skin. They show that the animal was reddish brown.

Borealopelta, the best-preserved armored dinosaur ever found

body armor plates

spine

Dinosaurs are often found by teams who go looking for them. But many are found by chance and often in unusual situations.

In 1993, a man was riding through the badlands of Patagonia, Argentina. He suddenly saw a giant leg bone sticking out of the sand! A team of scientists rushed there to see what else they could find.

This accidental discovery turned out to be a big find. This new species was large enough to rival the famous *T. rex*. It is the largest meat-eating dinosaur ever found in the southern part of Earth.

Giganotosaurus carolinii, named in honor of Ruben Carolini, who first spotted part of the skeleton in the sand

Dinosaurs of Australia and Antarctica

More than 100 million years ago, Australia and Antarctica were joined together. Here are some of the dinosaurs that lived on this ancient land.

Leaellynasaura
This dinosaur was used to living in the cold and dark. It had large eyes to help it see.

Cryolophosaurus
This theropod was the first Antarctic dinosaur named, in 1994. It had an unusual crest on its head.

Wintonotitan
One of Australia's most complete sauropods, its bones were found in 1974. It was originally nicknamed Clancy!

Kunbarrasaurus
This armored dinosaur wasn't one of the smartest. It had an unusually small brain compared to the size of its body.

Muttaburrasaurus
This dinosaur may have been able to blow air into the crest on its nose to inflate it and make loud noises.

Glossary

Ancestor
An animal or plant to which a more recent animal or plant is related

Badlands
A vast area of land that is often dry, rocky, and difficult to access

Camouflage
Colors or patterns on an animal's skin, fur, or feathers that help it merge with the environment

Embryo
An unborn or unhatched animal

Fossil
Remains or traces of a once-living animal or plant

Paleontologist
A scientist who studies prehistoric life through the examination of fossils

Prehistoric
An ancient time before recorded history

Quill
A stiff, sharp part of a feather or spine

Ravine
A deep, narrow valley

Sand dune
A hill of sand

Sauropod
A group of dinosaurs with long necks and tails

Theropod
A group of meat-eating dinosaurs that stood on two legs

Index

Quiz

Answer the questions to see what you have learned. Check your answers in the key below.

1. What is a paleontologist?

2. Which dinosaur was named for the three horns on its skull?

3. Which fossil was one of the first to show a close link between dinosaurs and birds?

4. What does *Deinocheirus* mean?

5. During what period of time did the first dinosaurs appear?

6. True or False: Some dinosaurs had feathers.

7. What makes heterodontosaurs unique among dinosaurs?

8. What is the largest dinosaur on record?

1. A person who studies dinosaurs and prehistoric life
2. *Triceratops* 3. *Archaeopteryx* 4. Terrible hand 5. Triassic period
6. True 7. Different types of teeth 8. *Argentinosaurus*

Eruption!

FIRST EDITION

Series Editor Deborah Lock; **Editor** Pomona Zaheer; **Art Editors** C. David Gillingwater, Dheeraj Arora; **Senior Art Editor** Clare Shedden; **US Editors** Regina Kahney, Shannon Beatty; **Production Editor** Siu Chan; **Producer, Pre-Production** Francesca Wardell; **Picture Researchers** Marie Osborn, Sumedha Chopra; **Jacket Designer** Natalie Godwin; **DTP Designer** Anita Yadav; **Managing Editor** Soma Chowdhury; **Managing Art Editor** Ahlawat Gunjan; **Indexer** Lynn Bresler; **Reading Consultant** Linda Gambrell, PhD

THIS EDITION

Editorial Management by Oriel Square
Produced for DK by WonderLab Group LLC
Jennifer Emmett, Erica Green, Kate Hale, *Founders*

Editors Grace Hill Smith, Libby Romero, Michaela Weglinski; **Photography Editors** Kelley Miller, Annette Kiesow, Nicole di Mella; **Managing Editor** Rachel Houghton; **Designers** Project Design Company; **Researcher** Michelle Harris; **Copy Editor** Lori Merritt; **Indexer** Connie Binder; **Proofreader** Larry Shea; **Reading Specialist** Dr. Jennifer Albro; **Curriculum Specialist** Elaine Larson

Published in the United States by DK Publishing
1745 Broadway, 20th Floor, New York, NY 10019

A catalog record for this book
is available from the Library of Congress.
ISBN: 978-0-5938-4255-3

DK books are available at special discounts when purchased
in bulk for sales promotions, premiums, fundraising, or
educational use. For details, contact: DK Publishing Special Markets,
1745 Broadway, 20th Floor, New York, NY 10019
SpecialSales@dk.com

Printed and bound in China

The publisher would like to thank the following for their kind permission to reproduce their images:
a=above; c=center; b=below; l=left; r=right; t=top; b/g=background

Alamy Stock Photo: Robertharding / Roberto Moiola 19tl, Science History Images 42, Westend61 GmbH / Fotofeeling 6-7; **Dorling Kindersley:** Jamie Marshall 18bl; **Dreamstime.com:** Ddkg 23tr, Evanfariston 22, Tearswept 36crb; **Getty Images:** Moment / Albert Damanik 20crb, Moment / Jose A. Bernat Bacete 21, Moment Open / by Mike Lyvers 19cr, Jim Sugar 1; **Shutterstock.com:** Dirk M. de Boer 43cra, cktravels.com 23b, Anton_Ivanov 29, James Davis Photography 27, Liudmila Legkaia 34-35, Rubi Rodriguez Martinez 18clb, Benny Marty 41b, Stephen Reich 4-5, Alfiya Safuanova 24tr, Lia Sanz 7crb

Cover image: *Front:* **Getty Images:** Jim Sugar; *Back:* **Dreamstime.com:** Ekaterina Mikhailova

All other images © Dorling Kindersley

www.dk.com

Eruption!

Anita Ganeri

Contents

Be a Volcano Ranger

Go on real adventures!

- ☑ Learn about volcanoes.
- ☑ Help to take care of volcano national parks.
- ☑ Share your learning with others.

Things you can do:

☑ Watch an eruption from a safe distance.

☑ Collect interesting volcanic rocks.

☑ Hike to the rim of an extinct volcano.

☑ Walk through extinct lava tubes.

volcanic rocks

What looks like a mountain but spits out fire? What shoots clouds of smoke from a hole in its top? What sometimes explodes with a **BANG?**

A volcano, and it's starting to erupt!

What Is a Volcano?

The story of a volcano starts underground. If you jump up and down on the ground, it feels solid and hard.

But far inside Earth, it is so hot that the rocks melt. The rocks are runny, like melted butter.

Sometimes, the melted rock, or magma, bursts up through a hole or a crack in the ground. This is how a volcano begins.

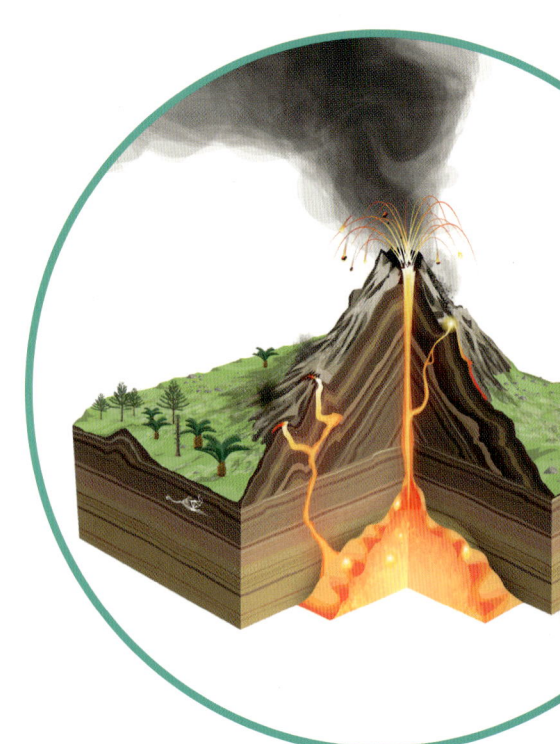

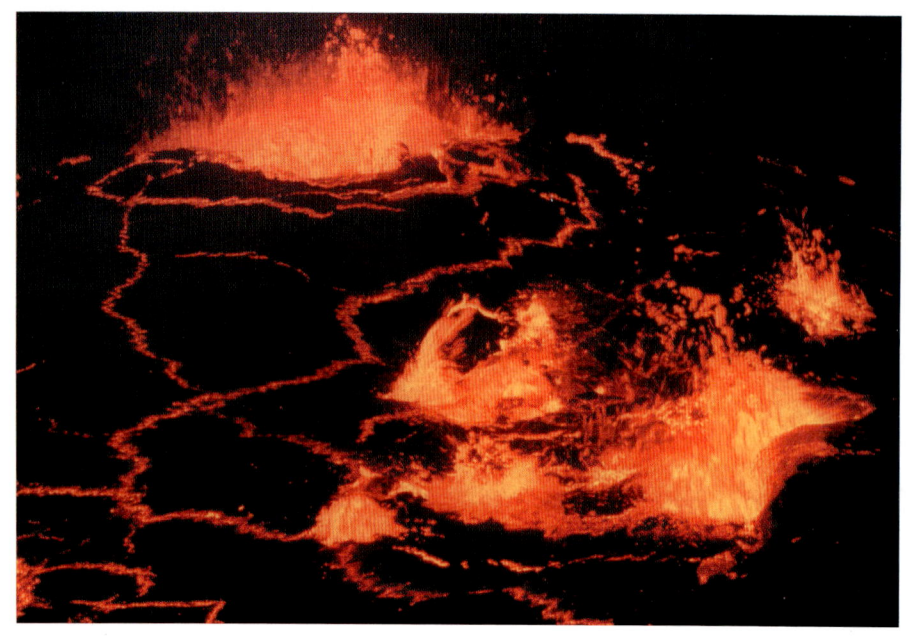

The melted rock that comes out of a volcano is called lava. At first, it is runny and red-hot. It cools down in the air and turns into hard, black rock.

Some volcanoes spurt out fiery fountains of lava. Other volcanoes pour out lava in great rivers of fire.

cooled lava

Once the lava starts flowing, nothing can stop it. It can bury whole villages and set trees and houses on fire.

Tectonic Plates
Earth's surface is made up of large slabs of moving rock called tectonic plates. These plates pull apart, slide past each other, and crash together. These movements can cause volcanoes to erupt and earthquakes to shake the ground.

Make a Volcano Model

To make an erupting cone-shaped volcano, you will need: a bottle, a tray, sand, baking soda, red food coloring, dishwashing liquid, and vinegar. You can decorate your volcano with plants, stones, and toy animals.

1. Place the bottle on the tray.

2. Build a mound of sand around the bottle. Keep the hole open.

3. Now place plants, stones, and toy animals around the volcano.

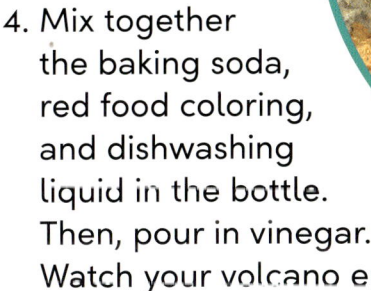

4. Mix together the baking soda, red food coloring, and dishwashing liquid in the bottle. Then, pour in vinegar. Watch your volcano erupt!

Types of Volcanoes

Volcanoes have different shapes and sizes. Some volcanoes erupt with a bang. Hot rocks and ash shoot high into the air. These volcanoes form cone-shaped mountains with steep sides.

Other volcanoes erupt quietly. The lava oozes gently out of the top and spreads out all around. These volcanoes are low and wide.

Cinder Cone Volcano

Cinder cone volcanoes spew lava that hardens and breaks into small pieces, or cinders. The falling cinders create a cone-shaped hill.

Composite Volcano

Composite volcanoes form as lava, ash, and cinders from previous eruptions build up over time. These large, steep volcanoes produce big explosions.

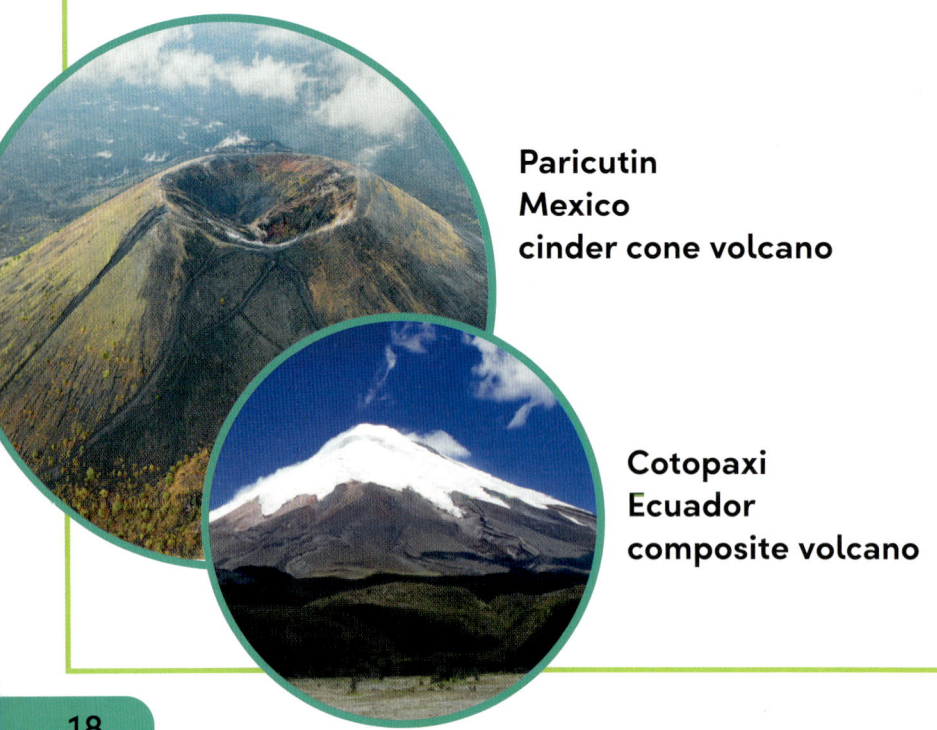

**Paricutin
Mexico
cinder cone volcano**

**Cotopaxi
Ecuador
composite volcano**

**Erta Ale
Ethiopia
shield volcano**

**Mount Lassen
California, USA
lava dome volcano**

Shield Volcano

The eruptions from a shield volcano are often slower than a composite's. Lava flows in all directions, creating wide slopes.

Lava Dome Volcano

Lava dome volcanoes form when lava is too thick to flow very far. The lava piles up over the volcano's opening, or vent.

Some volcanoes erupt violently. They blast out clouds of hot ash and dust. The ash is made of gas and tiny pieces of lava and rock.

Ash

It can be fine and powdery, or coarse like sand. Clouds of ash can travel thousands of miles away from a volcano. In 1815, when Mount Tambora in Indonesia erupted, ash spread around the world. It blocked the summer sun and caused parts of the planet to cool for several months.

The ash and dust shoot high into the air. Some of it lands near the volcano. It covers buildings and fields in thick, dark gray powder.

Some ash and dust is carried away by the wind. It can block out the sun and seem to turn day into night.

At the top of a volcano is a hollow called a crater. In it is a hole called the vent. Lava, ash, and dust come out of the vent. Some craters are many miles wide.

When a volcano stops erupting, the crater is left. Some old craters fill up with water to form huge lakes. Sometimes, the crater becomes a dry, grassy plain.

Crater Lake

Crater Lake in Oregon, USA, is the deepest lake in the United States. It formed when Mount Mazama, a volcano, erupted and then collapsed almost 8,000 years ago.

New Zealand's Emerald Lakes are crater lakes, too.

Stromboli

Lava shoots out of Stromboli,
a volcano located off the coast
of southern Italy, several times an hour.
Stromboli is nicknamed the "lighthouse of
the Mediterranean" because its fiery plumes
can be seen from far away at night.

When a volcano shoots out lava and ash, we say that it is erupting. We call a volcano that is erupting "active."

Kilauea (KILL-uh-WAY-uh) in Hawaii is the most active volcano on Earth. It has erupted nonstop since 1983!

We call a volcano that is not erupting "dormant." That means it is sleeping, but it could erupt at any time.

Montserrat is a tiny island in the Caribbean Sea. It used to be a beautiful place to live. Then, in 1995, a volcano called Chance's Peak started to erupt.

volcanic ash

It had been dormant for more than 300 years. Many people had to leave their homes as ash fell everywhere. Some left the island and went to live in another country. It was too dangerous for them to stay.

Mount Vesuvius (vuh-SOO-vee-uss) is a volcano in Italy. In 79 CE, Mount Vesuvius erupted violently, blasting hot ash and gas into the air.

The ash buried the town of Pompeii (pom-PAY) and thousands of people died. Today, you can walk around the streets of Pompeii and see the Roman ruins.

A cast of a dog covered by the ash

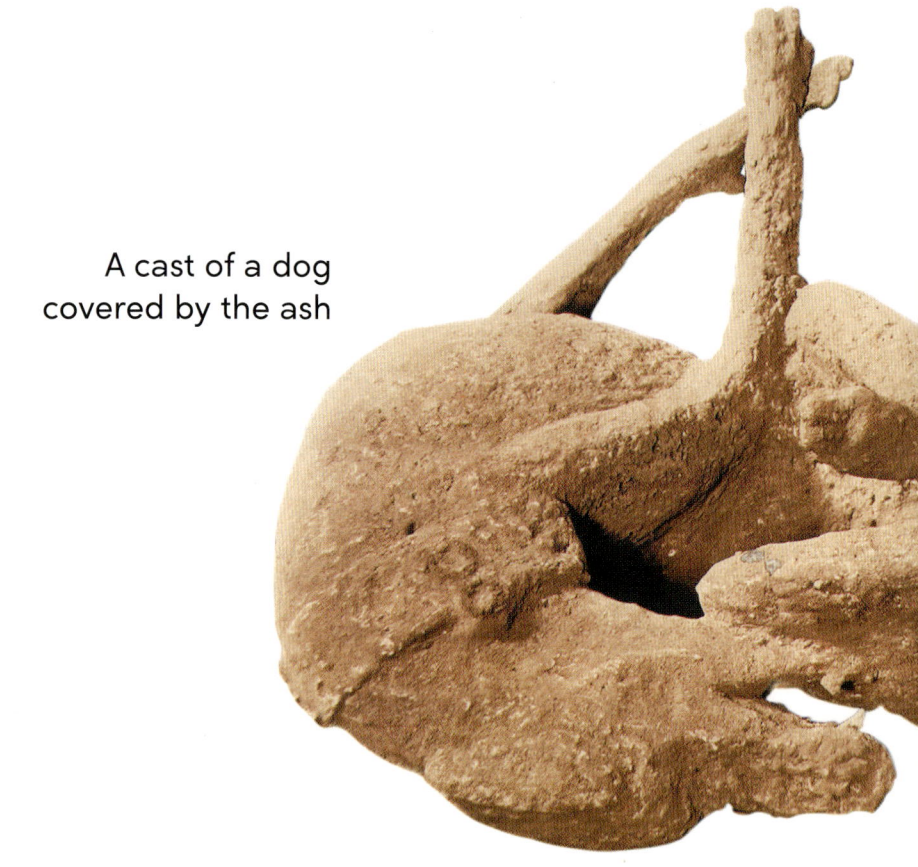

The ruins of the Roman town of Pompeii

Record Holders

Many volcanoes are famous for their eruptions and size. Here are some of the record holders.

Name: Mount Fuji
[Mount FOO-gee]

Location: Japan

Record: the world's most closely watched volcano

Name: Mount Vesuvius
[Mount vuh-SOO-vee-us]

Location: Italy

Record: the world's most visited volcano

Name: Mauna Loa
[MAW-nuh LOW-uh]

Location: Hawaii, USA

Record: the biggest
volcano on Earth

Active

Name: Krakatoa
[CRACK-uh-TOE-uh]

Location: Indonesia

Record: produced the
loudest bang ever heard
when it erupted in 1883

Active

Name: Kilauea
[KILL-uh-WAY-uh]

Location: Hawaii, USA

Record: the most active
volcano on Earth

Extinct

Name: Olympus Mons
[uh-LIM-puhs mons]

Location: Mars

Record: the biggest
volcano in the
known universe

Volcanoes: The Bad and the Good

Volcanoes can be very dangerous and set off other disasters.

Earthquake

A volcano can sometimes set off an earthquake. Violent earthquakes can destroy cities and kill people.

Tsunami

A volcanic eruption can cause a giant water wave called a tsunami. The wave destroys everything in its way.

Weather Disruption

When a volcano erupts, gas and dust are thrown up. This can blot out the sunlight and cause strong winds and heavy rainfall.

pumice stone

However, they can also be useful.

Rocks
Some volcanic rocks, such as pumice, can be used to rub away hard skin. Basalt is used to make building blocks and sidewalks.

Farming
Eruptions clear away old, dead plants. Volcanic ash makes the soil rich for strong and healthy plant growth.

Hot Springs
In some volcanic regions, people use hot underground water to heat their homes and make electricity.

Buried Treasure

Diamonds can be found in a type of rock called kimberlite. This rock is formed from a rare kind of magma found way below Earth's surface. When some volcanoes erupt, they can carry these buried treasures to the top!

In some places, blocks of solid lava are used to build roads, bridges, and houses. Precious gold and diamonds are found in some volcanic rock.

Near a volcano, the underground rocks get very hot. The hot rocks heat up water, which turns to steam. Sometimes, a giant jet of boiling water and steam bursts up through the ground and into the air. The jet is called a geyser.

Old Faithful is a famous geyser in Yellowstone Park, Wyoming, USA. It got its name because it bursts up about 20 times a day.

Soaking It In

Volcanic hot springs, like geysers, come from heat inside Earth. This is called geothermal heat. In Iceland's Blue Lagoon, people can soak in water that is heated by lava fields. And in Japan, macaques, or snow monkeys, can relax in hot springs, too!

There are lots of volcanoes under the sea.
You can't see most of them. But some
underwater volcanoes are so tall that they
poke up from the sea to make islands.

In 1963, a volcano erupted under the sea
near Iceland. The sea started to smoke
and steam. Not long after, the volcano
had grown and a brand-new island had
formed. The local people called it Surtsey,
named after an Icelandic fire god.

Ring of Fire

Most of Earth's active volcanoes are located underwater along the edges of the Pacific Ocean. Called the Ring of Fire, this is actually a horseshoe-shaped area with more than 450 volcanoes.

Hawaii is a group of more than 100 islands in the Pacific Ocean. The islands are the tops of huge underwater volcanoes. Some of these volcanoes have two or more craters, but they erupt very gently.

In some places, lava flows into the sea and makes it hiss and steam. Some of the beaches have black sand, which is made from crushed-up lava.

Lava Tubes

Hawaii has a lot of lava tubes, underground passages created by flowing lava. These tubes can be active, meaning that lava still flows. An extinct lava tube does not have flow. The lava cooled and formed a cavelike tunnel.

Volcanologists are scientists who try to find out how volcanoes work. They want to know when volcanoes are going to erupt. Then, people living nearby can be moved to safety.

But volcanologists have not found all the answers yet. No one knows when a volcano will erupt—until it actually does!

At Work

Volcanologists measure a volcano's temperature changes and monitor the gases that come out of it. These scientists also use equipment that detects tremors, or movements, in Earth's crust.

Animal Detectors

In 2012, scientists noticed that just hours before Mount Etna in Italy erupted, goats became nervous and ran away. The scientists think that the animals may have been able to feel early rumbles from the ground and detect gases in the air.

Volcanic Myths

In myths, volcanic eruptions are caused by gods and goddesses.

Vulcan

In Roman myths, he is the god of fire and crafts. The word "volcano" comes from his name. Vulcan's Greek name is Hephaestus.

In myths, he hides away in his workshops, which are under volcanoes. There, he heats and shapes metals.

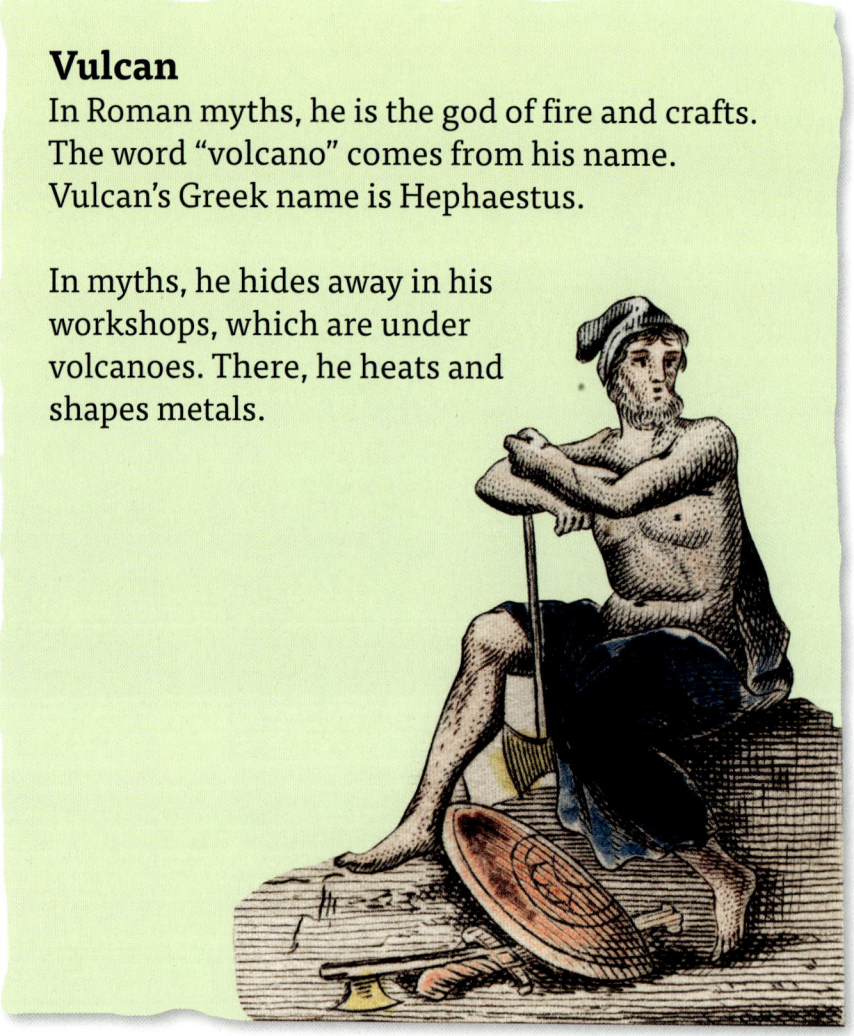

Pele

She is the Hawaiian goddess of volcanoes. The legends say that a volcano erupts when Pele gets angry.

Surtur

He is the Norse god of fire. The volcanic island of Surtsey is named after him.

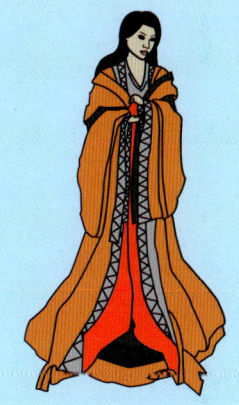

Fuchi

She is the Japanese goddess of fire. Mount Fuji is named after her.

Glossary

Active
A volcano that erupts

Ash
Tiny pieces of volcanic rock

Crater
A dip at the opening of a volcano where gas, lava, and ash come out

Dormant
A volcano that has not erupted in a long time but will erupt again

Eruption
When lava and ash shoot out of a volcano

Extinct
A volcano that has stopped erupting and will not erupt again

Geyser
A sudden jet of boiling water and steam

Lava
Hot, melted rock that comes out of a volcano

Tsunami
A giant wave of water that can be caused by volcanic eruptions or earthquakes

Vent
A volcano's opening

Volcanologist
(VUL-can-AHL-uh-gist)
A scientist who studies volcanoes

Index

Quiz

Answer the questions to see what you have learned. Check your answers in the key below.

1. Where does a volcanic eruption start?

2. What is the melted rock that comes out of a volcano called?

3. What is the hollow at the top of a volcano called?

4. Which is the most active volcano on Earth?

5. What type of volcano forms when lava, ash, and cinders from previous eruptions build up over time?

6. What type of volcano forms when lava is too thick to flow very far?

7. True or False: There are lots of volcanoes under the sea.

8. What are scientists who study volcanoes called?

1. Underground 2. Lava 3. A crater 4. Kilauea 5. A composite volcano 6. A lava dome volcano 7. True 8. A volcanologist

SAVE the CLIMATE

THIS EDITION
Editorial Management by Oriel Square
Produced for DK by WonderLab Group LLC
Jennifer Emmett, Erica Green, Kate Hale, *Founders*

Editors Grace Hill Smith, Libby Romero, Maya Myers, Michaela Weglinski;
Photography Editors Kelley Miller, Annette Kiesow, Nicole di Mella; **Managing Editor** Rachel Houghton;
Designers Project Design Company; **Researcher** Michelle Harris; **Copy Editor** Lori Merritt;
Indexer Connie Binder; **Proofreader** Larry Shea; **Reading Specialist** Dr. Jennifer Albro;
Curriculum Specialist Elaine Larson

Published in the United States by DK Publishing
1745 Broadway, 20th Floor, New York, NY 10019

Copyright © 2023 Dorling Kindersley Limited
DK, a Division of Penguin Random House LLC
24 25 26 27 28 10 9 8 7 6 5 4 3 2 1
001–341825–Mar/2024

A catalog record for this book
is available from the Library of Congress.
ISBN: 978-0-5938-4255-3

DK books are available at special discounts when purchased in bulk for sales promotions, premiums,
fundraising, or educational use. For details, contact: DK Publishing Special Markets,
1745 Broadway, 20th Floor, New York, NY 10019
SpecialSales@dk.com

Printed and bound in China

The publisher would like to thank the following for their kind permission to reproduce their images:
a=above; c=center; b=below; l=left; r=right; t=top; b/g=background

123RF.com: Witold Kaszkin 19cra, nerthuz 3cb, yasonya 23t; **Alamy Stock Photo:** Robertharding / Tony Waltham 10; **Dreamstime.
com:** Valentin M Armianu 9, Darren Baker 29, Ali Ender Birer 1cb, Galuniki 28br, Štěpán Kápl 20crb, Karynf4 22, Andrey Koturanov
12bl, Glenn Rogers 17tl, Rosshelen 26b, Toa555 16b, Vlabos 11br; **Getty Images:** Digital Vision / Lauren Nicole 17br, Jim Dyson 25t,
LightRocket / SOPA Images 24t, Stone / TED MEAD 13br; **Getty Images / iStock:** amriphoto 8bl, appledesign 4-5, Neurobite 18-19t;
Shutterstock.com: AleksandarMilutinovic 7crb, ArchonCodex 13tl, aydngvn 6-7, Olga Miltsova 27tr, Wildeside 12br, Ziablik 14-15l;

Cover images: *Front:* **Shutterstock.com:** FloridaStock

All other images © Dorling Kindersley
For more information see: www.dkimages.com

www.dk.com

MIX
Paper | Supporting
responsible forestry
FSC™ C018179
www.fsc.org

This book was made with Forest
Stewardship Council™ certified
paper - one small step in DK's
commitment to a sustainable future.
**For more information go to
www.dk.com/our-green-pledge**

SAVE the CLIMATE

Jen Szymanski

Contents

How Is Our Planet Changing?

A day at the beach is always a treat. But what if you arrived and saw this? The clear blue water you were expecting is foamy and brown. You can see gloopy patches of slime floating on top of the waves. The ocean is covered with sea snot! Yuck! Why is this happening?

The ocean is getting warmer, and it is changing. And it's not just the oceans. Temperatures all around Earth are on the rise. This is causing all sorts of changes to take place. Glaciers are melting. Sea levels are rising. Droughts and floods are becoming more common. Scientists believe all of this is happening because of climate change.

Slimy Waters
Sea snot isn't the same stuff that comes out of your nose when you have a cold. This slime is made by algae when ocean water gets warmer.

Climate is the pattern of weather in an area over a period of years. It includes things like how much snow and rain a place gets and how high and low the temperatures are there.

Climate change is a change in the usual weather patterns for a place. It can also be an overall change in Earth's climate. One example of climate change is a change in the average temperature for a place during a certain time of year. Another example is a change in the amount of rain or snow an area typically receives.

Weather or Climate?
The difference between weather and climate is time. Weather is what atmospheric conditions are like over a short period of time. Climate is how the atmosphere behaves over a long period of time.

The Sahara has one of the driest climates on Earth.

Briksdal Glacier, Norway
2002

Briksdal Glacier, Norway
2011

Earth's climate has always changed over time. That's nothing new. But the way Earth's climate is changing now is different, and scientists think people are to blame.

Scientists have lots of evidence that Earth's climate isn't the same as it was in the past. One obvious sign of that is global warming. Temperatures in most places on Earth have gone up about 1.8° F (1° C) in the past few centuries. That might not sound like a lot, but it's enough to cause a lot of changes.

A slight increase in Earth's average temperature causes ice and snow to melt. It causes glaciers to shrink. Glaciers all over the world have been melting more quickly. Some have disappeared completely.

All of that water from melting glaciers has to go somewhere. It runs down the slopes of hills and mountains and flows into the sea. It's a big reason the sea level rises every year. Scientists think the sea will rise along the United States coast at least 12 inches (0.3 m) by 2050.

As the sea level rises, the landscape changes. Land washes away. Coastlines move inland as oceans expand. Homes and buildings on the coast flood. They can be lost to the sea.

drought

flood

Changes in Ecosystems

Water running downhill picks up soil and carries it into streams and rivers. The dirt makes the water cloudy. This makes it harder for fish to breathe in the water.

While there is too much water in some places, there is too little in others. Long periods with no rain cause droughts. Plants, animals, and people often can't get enough water.

When the land is this dry, wildfires are a problem. Wildfires can be triggered by a bolt of lightning or a careless person building a fire. In recent years, wildfires fed by the dry land have become bigger and more frequent than ever before.

Worst Wildfire Season

Australia had its worst wildfire season ever in 2020. Billions of animals lost their homes.

Why Is Climate Change Happening?

Of all the planets in our solar system, Earth is the only one we know of that has life. Part of the reason for that is Earth's atmosphere.

As the Sun's energy passes through Earth's atmosphere, some of that energy is absorbed by Earth's surface. Some of that energy gets released as heat that rises back into the atmosphere.

The atmosphere is made of a mixture of gases. These gases act like a blanket. They trap the rising heat next to Earth's surface. This keeps the planet warm enough to support different kinds of life. But if there is too much of certain gases, problems arise.

One of the gases that traps heat is called carbon dioxide. For a long time, the amount of carbon dioxide in Earth's atmosphere remained pretty steady. But over the past century, it began to rise very rapidly.

Why the increase? It all started about 300 years ago. That was the beginning of the Industrial Revolution, which ushered in a flood of new inventions. Over time, these inventions led to coal-powered factories, steam engines, and gasoline-powered automobiles. All of these things burned fossil fuels, such as coal, oil, and natural gas, for energy. Burning fossil fuels releases carbon dioxide into the atmosphere.

The word "smog" comes from putting together parts of the words "smoke" and "fog."

Today, there are more cars and more factories. There's also much more carbon dioxide in the atmosphere than there was 100 years ago. When sunlight reacts with that carbon dioxide, other gases, and fine particles in the atmosphere, it forms smog. Smog turns the sky gray. It can make people sick, and it can kill plants.

Fossil Fuels
Fossil fuels come from ancient living things. When these organisms died, they were buried under layers of dirt and mud. Over millions of years, heat and pressure changed their remains into fossils.

Strangely, the part of Earth seeing the biggest impact from all of this is a place that has few cars—the Arctic. Temperatures there are rising about three times faster than the rest of the planet.

The Arctic's ice and snow reflect the Sun's energy. This helps to keep Earth's temperatures from getting too high. But as Arctic ice melts, more land is uncovered to release heat. Temperatures rise.

Land not covered by ice in the Arctic is covered by permafrost. This is a thick layer of soil under the surface that remains frozen. Higher temperatures warm the ground so the permafrost thaws. A gas called methane escapes the soft ground and rises into the atmosphere. Like carbon dioxide, methane traps heat. That causes Earth's temperature to creep up even more.

What Are People Doing About Climate Change?

Fortunately, scientists have lots of ideas about how to tackle the problem of climate change. At the top of their list is trying to decrease the amount of carbon dioxide entering Earth's atmosphere. One way to do this is to use new sources of energy that do not rely on fossil fuels. Another is to create new inventions that limit the amount of carbon dioxide released in the atmosphere.

Solar Panels
Solar panels absorb energy from the Sun and change it into electric energy. Wires carry the electricity away from solar panels to homes and businesses.

The spinning blades of a wind turbine turn energy from the wind into electricity.

A big step is using more renewable energy sources to make electricity. Tapping into energy from the Sun, wind, and water releases less carbon dioxide than burning fossil fuels.

The possibilities are amazing. Many new cars, for example, run on electricity. Other cars, buses, and airplanes are powered by fuels made from algae, sugar, and even cooking oil!

Limiting new carbon dioxide emissions is one thing. But how do you take out a gas that's already in the atmosphere? Fortunately, nature has already given us a tool to help conquer that problem—plants!

Plants take carbon dioxide out of the atmosphere and use it to make energy. Replanting forests that have been cut down is one way to soak up some of the carbon dioxide. Planting gardens is another. Garden plants need carbon dioxide to grow, too. And, when more people grow their own vegetables, fewer trucks are needed to carry food from farms to stores. That's a win-win!

What Can You Do About Climate Change?

Despite everything that's being done to fight climate change, there's one more huge challenge. How do you make people understand that climate change is a massive and urgent problem?

The atmosphere surrounds the entire planet. It doesn't matter where extra carbon dioxide comes from. It all ends up in the same place. And it all adds up to one huge problem for Earth.

Greta Thunberg is a climate activist from Sweden. In 2018, she started an international movement to fight climate change.

One thing you can do is to make other people aware of the problem. Help them understand how they can make a difference. Knowledge and awareness are powerful tools in stopping climate change.

Have you ever heard the expression "going green"? Many people say that's what we need to do to save Earth's climate. All it means is changing your own everyday habits to cut down on the amount of carbon dioxide entering Earth's atmosphere.

The easiest thing you can do is to use less energy. Turn off lights when you leave a room. Turn off the TV when you are done watching it. Both of these actions can help your household use less electricity—and save money, too.

What About Water?

Moving water to homes and making it safe to drink takes energy. Turn off the water when you brush your teeth, and take a shorter shower to save energy.

Making new things like clothes and electronics takes energy. You can make a difference by buying used things. Or, you can fix things that are broken rather than throwing them away. Your choices count.

Scientists use the term "carbon footprint" to describe how much carbon dioxide each person generates when they use energy. Choices to use less energy make your carbon footprint smaller.

What choices will you make? Someday, you may choose a career in which you help to solve the problem of climate change. You might be a scientist who discovers a fuel that doesn't release carbon dioxide. Or, you might make an invention that easily absorbs extra carbon dioxide right out of the atmosphere.

In the meantime, learn all you can about the problem. Inspire others to help. And you, too, can do your part to save the climate!

Biggest Carbon Footprints
Highly populated countries like China and the U.S. have the largest total carbon footprints. Some small countries like Qatar and New Caledonia have the largest carbon footprints per person.

Glossary

Absorbed
Soaked up

Atmosphere
A thick layer of gases that surrounds Earth

Carbon dioxide
A colorless gas made of carbon and oxygen that helps trap heat next to Earth

Carbon footprint
The amount of carbon dioxide produced by a person by using energy

Climate
The average weather conditions in an area over a period of years

Drought
A long period with little or no rainfall

Evidence
The information, observation, or facts that support a claim

Fossil fuels
Fuels such as coal, oil, or natural gas made from the remains (fossils) of ancient plants and animals

Glaciers
Slow-moving rivers of ice formed at Earth's poles and on mountaintops

Global warming
The slow increase of Earth's temperature due to extra carbon dioxide in the atmosphere

Permafrost
A layer of soil found near Earth's poles that is always frozen

Reflect
To bounce off

Renewable resource
A resource that can't get used up

Smog
Air pollution made of gases and fine particles

Weather
The conditions in the atmosphere at a specific point in time

Index

Quiz

Answer the questions to see what you have learned. Check your answers in the key below.

1. True or False: Weather and climate are the same thing.

2. Are some changes in climate normal?

3. Are the climate changes we are seeing now normal?

4. What does climate change cause that leads to more wildfires?

5. How does too much carbon dioxide in the atmosphere cause climate change?

6. True or False: Energy from the Sun, wind, and water releases as much carbon dioxide as burning coal or oil.

7. What can people do to get rid of excess carbon dioxide in the atmosphere?

8. What do you do when you "go green"?

1. False 2. Yes 3. No 4. Drought 5. Carbon dioxide traps heat next to Earth, and this makes the temperature of Earth's surface get warmer 6. False 7. Plant trees and other kinds of plants 8. Change your everyday habits

Twisters

FIRST EDITION
Project Editor Louise Pritchard; **Art Editor** Jill Plank; **US Editor** Regina Kahney; **Production** Siu Chan;
Picture Researcher Liz Moore; **Jacket Designer** Natalie Godwin; **Illustrator** Peter Dennis;
Publishing Manager Bridget Giles; **Reading Consultant** Linda Gambrell, PhD

THIS EDITION
Editorial Management by Oriel Square
Produced for DK by WonderLab Group LLC
Jennifer Emmett, Erica Green, Kate Hale, *Founders*

Editors Grace Hill Smith, Libby Romero, Michaela Weglinski;
Photography Editors Kelley Miller, Annette Kiesow, Nicole DiMella; **Managing Editor** Rachel Houghton;
Designers Project Design Company; **Researcher** Michelle Harris; **Copy Editor** Lori Merritt;
Indexer Connie Binder; **Proofreader** Larry Shea; **Reading Specialist** Dr. Jennifer Albro;
Curriculum Specialist Elaine Larson

Published in the United States by DK Publishing
1745 Broadway, 20th Floor, New York, NY 10019

Copyright © 2023 Dorling Kindersley Limited
DK, a Division of Penguin Random House LLC
24 25 26 27 28 10 9 8 7 6 5 4 3 2 1
001–341825–Mar/2024

A catalog record for this book
is available from the Library of Congress.
ISBN: 978-0-5938-4255-3

DK books are available at special discounts when purchased
in bulk for sales promotions, premiums, fundraising, or
educational use. For details, contact: DK Publishing Special Markets,
1745 Broadway, 20th Floor, New York, NY 10019
SpecialSales@dk.com

Printed and bound in China

The publisher would like to thank the following for their kind permission to reproduce their images:
a=above; c=center; b=below; l=left; r=right; t=top; b/g=background

123RF.com: solarseven 1; **Alamy:** Steve Morgan 14, Reuters / Rick Wilking 26–27b, John Sirlin 14;
Dreamstime.com: Andrey Armyagov 29cra, Kelpfish 28–29, Lastdays1 24; **Planet Earth Pictures:** Paolo Fanciulli 9, Alex Benwell 15;
Robert Harding Picture Library: Warren Faidley/Int'l Stock 16–17, 18cl, Beougher 18 br; **Shutterstock:** Minerva Studio 4–5,
Ernest R. Prim 24, Joe Belanger 26–27; **Tony Stone Images:** 20b, Christoph Burki 7tr, Alan R Moller 19; **Topham Picturepoint:** 25

Cover images: *Front:* **Dreamstime.com:** Solarseven; *Back:* **Dreamstime.com:** Macrovector Art cla, Tarasdubov cl, cra

All other images © Dorling Kindersley Limited

www.dk.com

MIX
Paper | Supporting
responsible forestry
FSC™ C018179

This book was made with Forest
Stewardship Council™ certified
paper - one small step in DK's
commitment to a sustainable future.
**For more information go to
www.dk.com/our-green-pledge**

Twisters

Kate Hayden

Contents

A Twister Tale

Rob was working in his farmyard in Texas, USA. It was a peaceful spring day. But his dog, Barney, was unhappy. He hid under a tractor and would not come out. Rob wondered if Barney was sick.

Second Sense
Animals have sharper senses than we have. Many can sense changes in the weather, like just before a bad storm.

Suddenly, the sky went dark. Hailstones as big as golf balls pelted down from the sky. Thunder rolled and lightning flashed. Then, came a deathly stillness in the air. Somehow, Barney had known!

A moment later, huge black clouds
began to spin. They bubbled at the top, like
boiling milk. Gusts of wind blew straw
around. Just then, a column of gray spiraled
down from the sky. A twister!

Rob stood rooted to the spot. The twister touched the ground. Mud and grass swirled up, like smoke from a bonfire. That was only the start. The twister began to move.
It skipped and bounced across the fields. It grew bigger, faster, and dirtier as it picked up mud from the ground.

Waterspouts
Twisters over bodies of water are called waterspouts. They whisk up water. The tallest one ever seen was a mile (1.6 km) high.

Suddenly, the twister was hanging right over Rob's farm. There was a noise like a rushing waterfall, then—BANG!
The barn exploded as if a bomb had gone off inside it.

Rob ran with Barney to the cellar in his house. His ears were hurting, and he could hardly breathe. That's because the air pressure around a twister is very low. The low pressure makes people's ears ache and causes buildings to explode.

Just as Rob reached the cellar, his front porch flew off with an earsplitting **CRASH!** Then came a **SMASH** as the house windows blew in. Two minutes later, all was silent.

Rob and his wife, Ann, came up from the cellar. Furniture lay smashed on the floor. Most of the doors and windows were gone. Rob and Ann felt lucky to be alive.

Neighbors helped them clean
up. The twister did not damage
the neighbors' houses.

Fast and Furious

funnel cloud

Twisters can form when cold air meets warm air. The warm air is sucked up in a swirling column called a funnel cloud. The cloud spins at a great speed. Twisters contain the most deadly winds in the world.

No one knows what a twister will do next. It can lift up a large truck and smash it to pieces but leave small objects undamaged.

A twister once picked up a baby boy and set him down safely 300 feet (91 m) away. The baby did not even wake up!

Strange Showers
When twisters drop things they've picked up, strange things can happen. A twister in England caused a shower of frogs.

There are lots of strange stories about twisters. A twister once blew away a man's birth certificate. The twister carried it 50 miles (80 km) and dropped it in a friend's garden.

Another twister sucked up some roses and water from a vase. It dropped them in another room. But it left the vase on the table.

One twister picked up a jar of pickles and carried the jar for miles without damaging it.

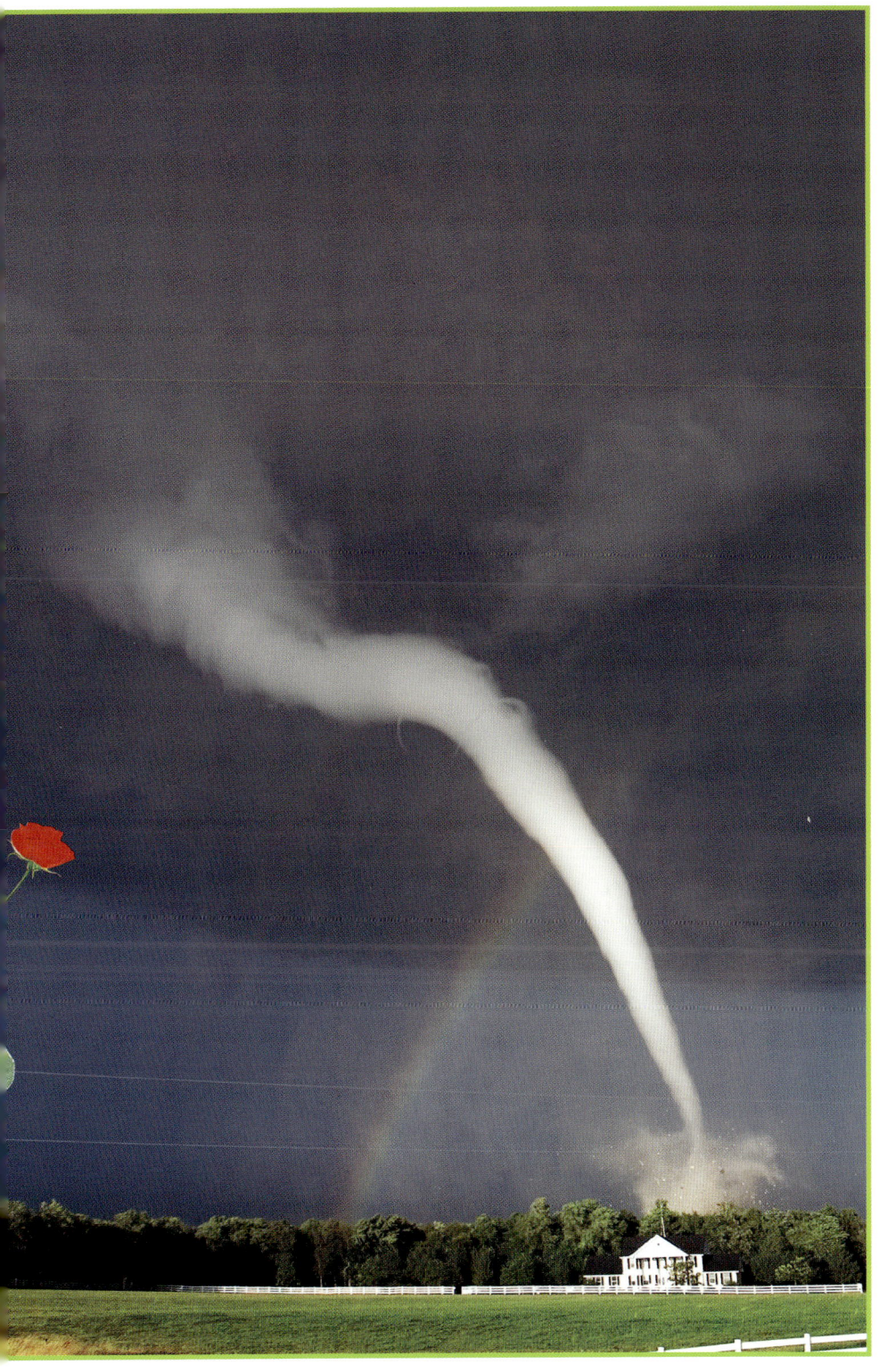

A Close Look

Twisters come in many different shapes and sizes. They can be thin, white, and wispy. Or they can be big, thick, and black.

They can even be in color. If a twister travels across a muddy field, the mud turns it brown—and very smelly!

Twisters can grow bigger and faster as they go along. Some look like they have a loop or knot in the middle.

Some are wider at the bottom than at the top. Some are shaped like a tube. Others look like a slice of pie.

Lots of people have seen
a twister from the outside.
But only a few have looked
inside a twister and survived.

A farmer named Will Keller once
looked up into a twister from his
underground shelter. Just as he closed
the door of his shelter, he saw lots of
mini twisters inside the big twister.
These mini twisters can rip through
a building and slice it to shreds.

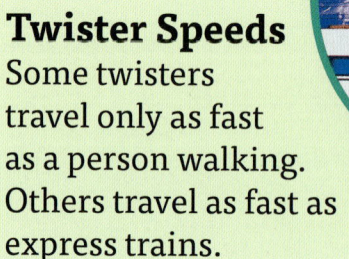

Twister Speeds
Some twisters
travel only as fast
as a person walking.
Others travel as fast as
express trains.

Tornado Country

Twisters are also known as tornadoes. There is an area in the central United States that is called Tornado Alley. It is famous for its deadly twisters. Many violent tornadoes occur in the southern USA as well.

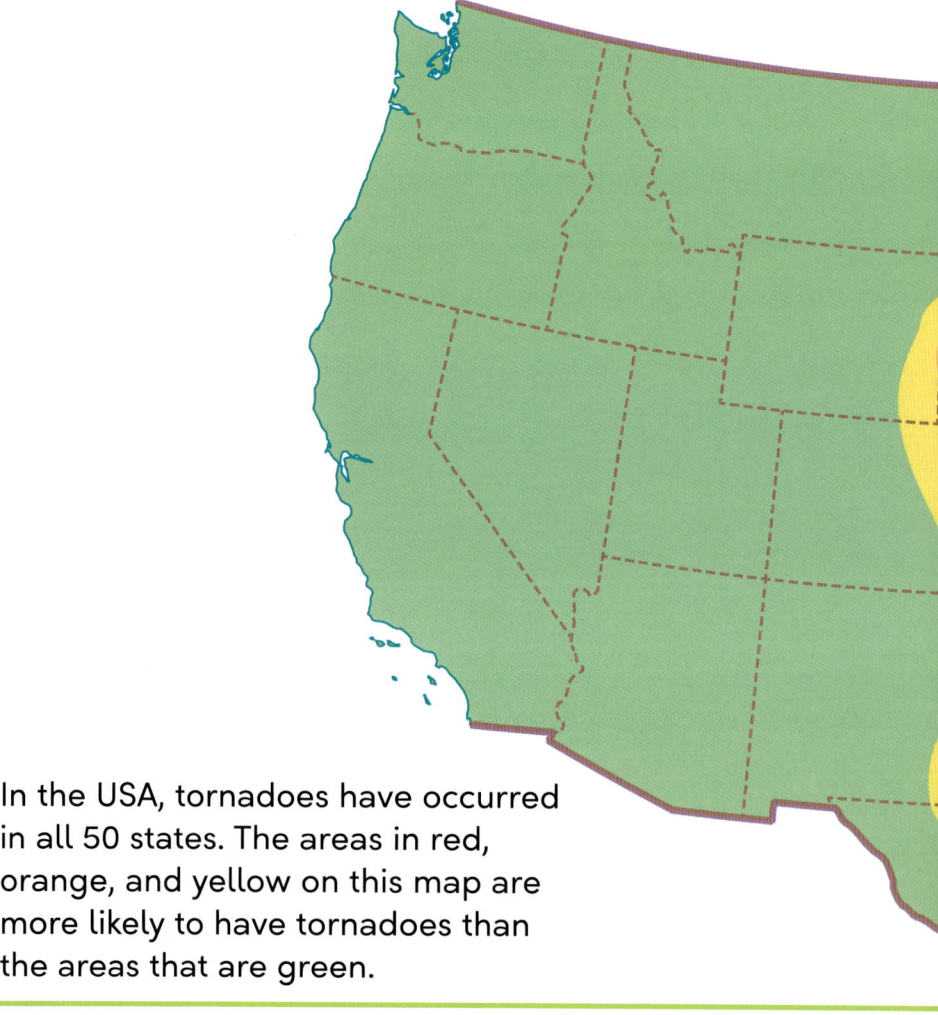

In the USA, tornadoes have occurred in all 50 states. The areas in red, orange, and yellow on this map are more likely to have tornadoes than the areas that are green.

Twisters typically form between April and July as warm air from the south meets cold air from the north—right over these parts of the USA.

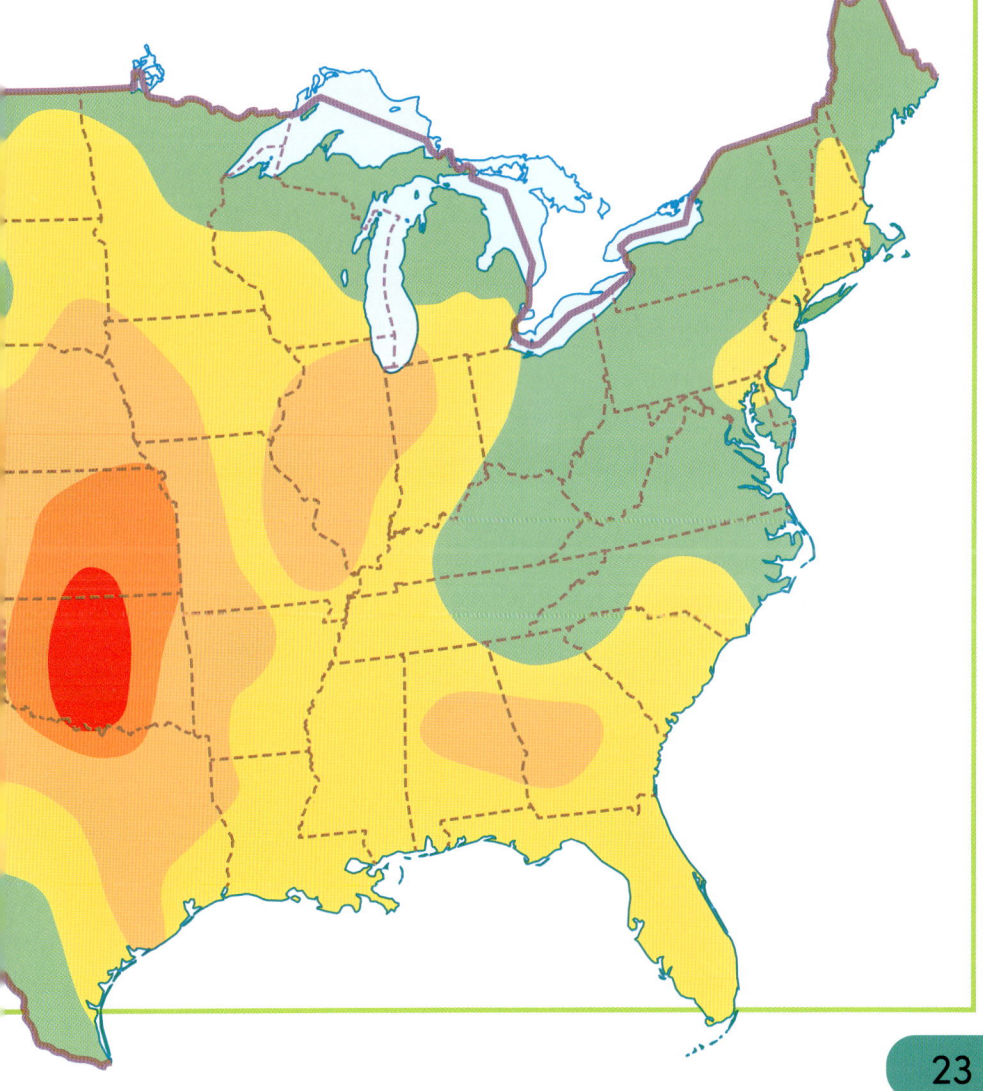

The Enhanced Fujita Scale measures a tornado's strength.

An EF0 damages chimneys.

An EF1 snaps telephone poles.

An EF2 rips off roofs.

An EF3 flips over trains.

An EF4 destroys even strong homes.

An EF5 leaves few things standing.

In 2013, an EF5 ripped through Moore, Oklahoma, USA.

It killed 24 people.

The Worst Twister
In 1925, one twister in Tornado Alley destroyed four towns in less than four hours. It killed 689 people.

People in Tornado Alley are well prepared for twisters. Many of them have an underground shelter outside their home.

The shelter gives people a safe place to wait until the tornado is gone.

People without a shelter hide in a cellar or small room in the middle of their house.

This shelter outside a home in Oklahoma City, Oklahoma, USA, has a stairway that leads to a small room underground.

Emergency Supplies

People keep emergency supplies in their shelters—food, drink, flashlights, and a first-aid kit.

The shelter was not damaged even after an EF5 tornado, the strongest of tornadoes, hit. The shelter kept nine people safe.

Tracking Twisters

Scientists use a computer to help them forecast twisters. The computer makes a picture that shows where a twister is and how fast it is traveling.

Some scientists follow a twister as it moves across the ground. Many of them use equipment such as a satellite dish.

In the past, people did not know when a twister was coming. Today, scientists give people time to find shelter, and hundreds of lives are saved.

Forecasts from Space
Scientists who study the weather are called meteorologists. Some satellites, which are spacecraft that orbit Earth, send information about the weather to these scientists.

Glossary

Cellar
A room or rooms built underground

Enhanced Fujita Scale
A scale that rates a tornado's strength

Forecast
To use information to predict what is likely to happen in the future

Funnel cloud
A swirling column of warm air

Hailstones
Small balls of ice that fall from storm clouds

Meteorologist
A scientist who studies the weather

Satellite
A spacecraft that orbits Earth to gather information

Tornado
Another word for twister

Waterspout
A tornado that occurs over a body of water

Index

Quiz

Answer the questions to see what you have learned. Check your answers in the key below.

1. How do twisters form?

2. What is the swirling column of air in a twister called?

3. True or False: Twisters form in only one shape.

4. What do you call a twister that forms over a body of water?

5. In which parts of the USA do many tornadoes occur?

6. Between what months do twisters typically form in the USA?

7. What is used to measure a tornado's strength?

8. What kind of scientist studies twisters?

1. Cold air meets warm air 2. A funnel cloud 3. False
4. A waterspout 5. Tornado Alley and the southern USA
6. April and July 7. The Enhanced Fujita scale 8. A meteorologist